Wild Britain

KT-558-480

Seashore

Louise and Richard Spilsbury

C151853217

www.heinemann.co.uk
Visit our website to find out more information about Heinemann Library books.

To order:
 Phone 44 (0) 1865 888066
 Send a fax to 44 (0) 1865 314091
Visit the Heinemann Bookshop at www.heinemann.co.uk to browse our catalogue and order online.

First published in Great Britain by Heinemann Library,
Halley Court, Jordan Hill, Oxford OX2 8EJ
a division of Reed Educational and Professional Publishing Ltd.
Heinemann is a registered trademark of Reed Educational & Professional Publishing Ltd.

OXFORD MELBOURNE AUCKLAND JOHANNESBURG BLANTYRE
GABORONE IBADAN PORTSMOUTH (NH) USA CHICAGO

© Reed Educational and Professional Publishing Ltd 2001
The moral right of the proprietor has been asserted.

All rights reserved. No part of this publication may be reproduced, stored in a retrieval system, or transmitted in any form or by any means, electronic, mechanical, photocopying, recording, or otherwise without either the prior written permission of the Publishers or a licence permitting restricted copying in the United Kingdom issued by the Copyright Licensing Agency Ltd, 90 Tottenham Court Road, London W1P 0LP.

Designed by Celia Floyd
Illustrations by Alan Fraser
Originated by Dot Gradations
Printed in Hong Kong/China

ISBN 0 431 03903 8 (hardback)   ISBN 0 431 03910 0 (paperback)
06 05 04 03 02 01   06 05 04 03 02 01
10 9 8 7 6 5 4 3 2   10 9 8 7 6 5 4 3 2 1

British Library Cataloguing in Publication Data
Spilsbury, Louise
   Seashore. – (Wild Britain)
   1. Seashore – Great Britain – Juvenile literature
   2. Seashore ecology – Great Britain – Juvenile literature
   I. Title II. Spilsbury, Richard
   577.6'99'0941

KENT ARTS & LIBRARIES	
C151853217	

Acknowledgements

To our own young wildlife enthusiasts, Miles and Harriet.

The Publishers would like to thank the following for permission to reproduce photographs:
Bruce Coleman: Jan van de Kam p16, Michael Glover p19, Jane Burton p23; Corbis/Ecoscene: Peter Hulme p7; Oxford Scientific Films: Ian West pp4, 29, G I Bernard pp5, 11, 14, 18, 24, David Cayless p6, David Thompson pp8, 9, London Scientific Films p10, Niall Benvie p12, 20, 22, Tony Bomford p15, Mark Hamblin pp17, 28, Rodger Jackman p21, Colin Milkins p25, Survival Anglia/Terry Andrewartha p26, Nobert Rosing p27; Wildlife Matters: p13

Cover photograph reproduced with permission of Images

Our thanks to Andrew Solway for his comments in the preparation of this book.

Every effort has been made to contact copyright holders of any material reproduced in this book. Any omissions will be rectified in subsequent printings if notice is given to the Publisher.

Contents

Any words appearing in the text in bold, **like this**, are explained in the Glossary.

What is a seashore?

The lower part of the seashore is covered in water most of the day. The top part is only covered for a short time.

The seashore is where the sea meets the land. Britain is made up of islands, so there are many seashores around the country.

A seashore habitat like this provides living things with food, water and **shelter**.

A **habitat** is the natural home of a group of plants and animals. In this book we will look at a few of the many different plants and animals that live, grow and **reproduce** in a seashore habitat.

Types of seashore

Water wears away the rocks and changes their shape.

There are two main types of seashore – rocky and sandy. Rocky seashores are covered in rocks that have broken off from the cliffs above.

Sand is made up of tiny pieces of rock and broken shells.

Rocks that fall into the sea are broken up by the waves. They break into smaller and smaller pieces to form pebbles and sand. The sea washes the sand onto the shore.

Changes

The high tide line is the highest place the water reaches up a seashore. Water covers the shore.

The seashore is always changing because of the **tides**. Twice a day the sea rises up the shore and then goes out again. High tide is when the sea comes up the shore.

At low tide the beach and rocks are uncovered.

Low tide is when the sea has gone back out again. On some seashores, like this one, the difference between high and low tides is great. On others it may be very little.

9

Living there

Under water barnacles open up and comb the water for tiny bits of food with their hairy feet.

Seashore creatures have to survive in a **habitat** that changes with the **tides**. Twice a day, when the tide is in, they move about and feed in the water.

Out of water, barnacles close up their shells for protection.

When the tide is out, their habitat is out of the water. Sea creatures have different ways of protecting themselves from drying out in hot sun or freezing in cold winds.

Seaweed

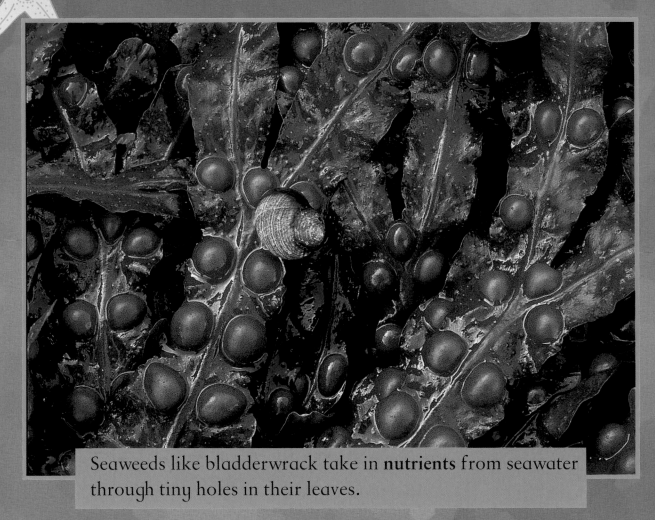

Seaweeds like bladderwrack take in **nutrients** from seawater through tiny holes in their leaves.

Different types of seaweed live at different levels of the seashore. Those high up the shore, like bladderwrack, can survive out of water for a long time.

Holdfasts stop seaweeds being washed away by moving water.

Some seaweeds, like kelp, cannot live for long out of water. They live lower down the shore. These seaweeds have an end called a holdfast. This attaches them firmly to rocks.

13

Life under the sand

Lugworms take **nutrients** from sand as they pass it through their bodies. Worm casts like this are the left-over sand.

Hundreds of animals live under the sand. There are shellfish, like cockles and razorshells, as well as sandworms and lugworms. They burrow into the sand when the **tide** goes out.

When the tide comes in, sand eels wriggle out of the sand to swim in groups and feed.

Animals hide under the sand to escape the hot sun and the wind, and the birds that eat them. As the tide comes in again, they come out of hiding to eat food carried in by the tide.

15

Animals on the seashore

A crab has ten legs. The two front legs have claws for fighting and picking up their food.

Crabs also dig into the sand to hide from seabirds that try to eat them. Crabs have shells that protect their soft bodies inside, in case waves knock them against rocks.

Common seals are shy. They rest on quiet shores away from people.

Common seals come on to sandy beaches to rest. They also have their pups (babies) on the shore. But they spend most of their time in the sea searching for fish to eat.

Life on the rocks

Limpets move around to graze on seaweed, then go back to the same bit of rock.

Some animals that live on rocks can stay out of the water for a long time. Limpets are sea snails. They suck tightly onto rocks under their pointed shell. This stops them from drying out in the sun or wind.

Sea anemones like this one sting tiny fish with their long **tentacles** before eating them.

Some animals, such as sea anemones, die if they dry out. They do not have a shell to hide under, so sea anemones live lower down the shore where they are underwater most of the time.

Life in rock pools

Blennies have speckled bodies that look like rocks. This **camouflages** them from birds that might eat them.

When the **tide** goes out, some water is left in dips in the rocks. Many different seaweeds and sea creatures live in rock pools. Blennies are small fish that feed on barnacles from the rocks.

Starfish have a mouth in the middle of the underside of their bodies.

Starfish also live in rock pools. Starfish use their five arms to force open mussel shells to eat the animal inside.

On the tide line

Sometimes jellyfish are washed up onto the tide line.

Lots of dead seaweed and sea creatures float about at sea. Some are washed on to the shore. Seaweed, rubbish and small animals are also left on the high **tide** line.

Sandhoppers feed on rotting seaweed on the high tide line.

Sandhoppers usually come out at night on the high tide line. They are a bit like woodlice. They need to live in a damp and shady **habitat**.

Beachcombing

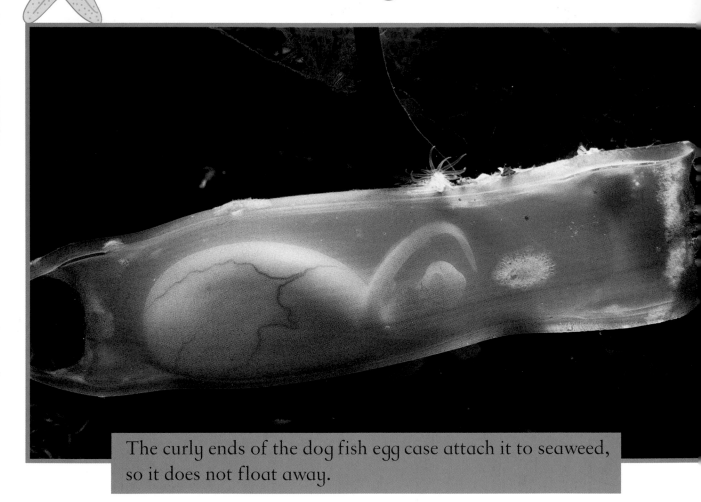

The curly ends of the dog fish egg case attach it to seaweed, so it does not float away.

Some sea fish lay their eggs in cases. The cases protect the baby fish until they **hatch** out. You often see empty fish egg cases washed up on the beach.

Sea mice, like this one, can be up to 20 cm long.

The sea mouse is not a mouse at all. It is a kind of sea-worm with a grey-brown hairy body. You sometimes see them washed up on the seashore.

Birds

The oystercatcher gets its name because it also eats oysters.
Oysters are shelled creatures a bit like mussels.

Many birds live and feed by the seashore.
The oystercatcher has a strong beak for
pulling open the shells of mussels and
cockles to eat the animals inside.

Herring gulls may eat the food they catch themselves, or take it to feed their young.

Herring gulls eat almost anything. They will snatch scraps from a family picnic or catch crabs, snails and small fish that live on the shore or in the sea.

Dangers

This seal is tangled in an old fishing net. Without help it may die.

The sea is so big, some people use it like a giant bin. The rubbish they throw in is washed up on to the seashore. **Pollution** can harm the living things on the seashore.

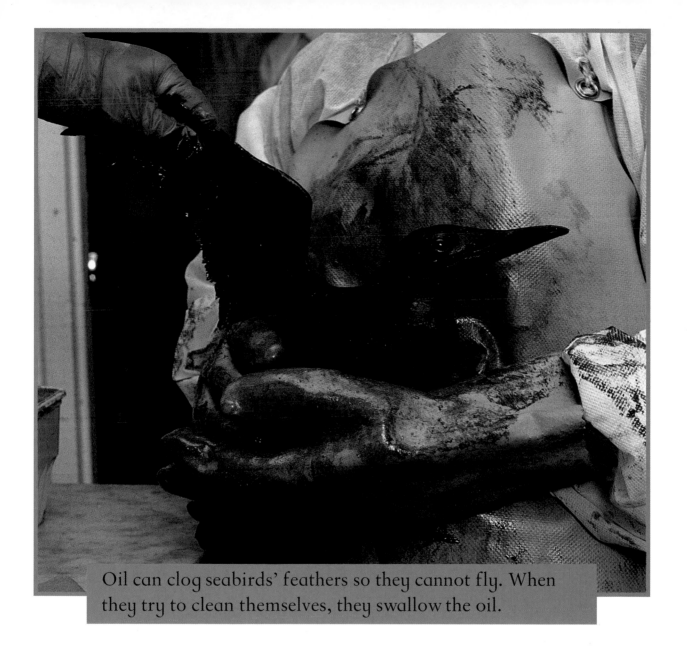

Oil can clog seabirds' feathers so they cannot fly. When they try to clean themselves, they swallow the oil.

When oil is spilled from ships at sea, it washes ashore. Oil spills can kill many of the living things on a seashore.

Food chains

A food chain shows the link between plants and animals in a **habitat**. There are many different food chains in a seashore habitat. Here is one example.

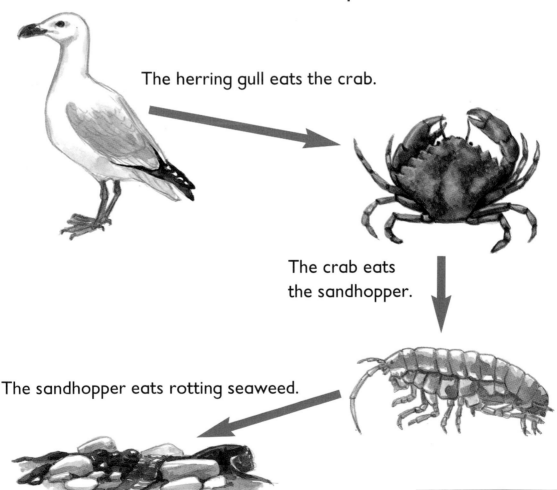

The herring gull eats the crab.

The crab eats the sandhopper.

The sandhopper eats rotting seaweed.

The artwork on this page is not to scale.

Glossary

camouflage when animals have colours or shapes that match their habitat and make them hard to see

habitat the natural home of a group of plants and animals

hatch to be born from an egg

nutrients food that gives living things the goodness they need to live and grow

pollution when air, water or land is poisoned or damaged

reproduce when plants and animals make young just like themselves

shelter somewhere safe to stay, live and have young

tentacles these are long and thin and are used for moving, feeling or grasping

tides high tide is when the sea rises up the beach; low tide is when it comes back down the beach

Index